TRADITIONAL CUISINE OF **MOROCCO**

Fabulous, delicious, tasty, refined, fascinating; no adjec
to describe all the riches of Moroccan cuisine, a cuisine tho
senses. Moroccan fare is refined in flavour, reflecting the stature of a deeply-
rooted culture whose delights are found in all the world's capitals.

A *tagine*, bringing together family and friends, creates a universe of hos-
pitality and fellowship. The sun shines from this cuisine, which emanates such
magic that we cannot help but love it. This is a cuisine largely prepared by
Moroccan women, with great love and skill.

This book, by Mou mini Bouchra, takes us into the heart of this universe,
with all its poetry. The author makes art of this splendid gastronomic mosaic, in
which each recipe is a tiny artwork that will delight our eyes and our palate
alike.

Mou mini Bouchra is our guide to the generous, welcoming world that sur-
rounds the hospitable Moroccan table.

This book is so appetizing that it is guaranteed to redouble our zest for
life itself!

Bravo! A thousand times bravo for this book, whose success is assured.

Kharchafi Med

TRADITIONAL CUISINE OF MOROCCO
© Text: Alami Talbi Othman
© Photographs: Seghrouchní Idrissi Youness
Cuisine and decoration: Mrs Moumini Bouchra
Colaboration: Alami Talbi Jaouad

Distribution:
Sté Distribution de Cartes Touristiques, 11 Angle Ali Bnou Talib et Hassane Ibn Tabit Champs de Course. Fès, Marruecos.
Tels: 212 (0) 61 06 22 03 - 212 (0) 64 85 33 07
Fax: 212 (0) 35 65 01 45
e-mail: ste.distribution.de.cartes.touristiques@hotmail.com
edition.alami@gmail.com

Diagrams and reproduction conceived and carried out in their entirety by the technical teams of
EDITORIAL FISA ESCUDO DE ORO, S.A.

I.S.B.N. 978-84-378-2542-7
Printed in Spain
Legal Dep. B. 20857-2013

INTRODUCTION

This book contains recipes for the most traditional dishes in Moroccan cuisine, a cuisine that, thanks to its wise use of ingredients and methods of cooking, is rightly considered one of the most refined in the world. These are traditions, too, which go back over a thousand years, the fruit of recipes passed down, in the main, from mother to daughter.

The principal ingredients in the cuisine of Morocco are provided by the rich fruits of the land and by lamb, beef or veal and chicken, as well as fish. This is, then, complete, nutritional fare. Its preparation is based on the harmonious mixture of sweet and salty flavours and, above all, on the use of spices, which give all these dishes a truly appetizing aroma and flavour. The most frequently used spices are black pepper, cumin, natural saffron, ginger, red pepper and cinnamon. Aromatic herbs also provide a finishing touch and additional flavour in the form, particularly, of parsley and coriander, always natural, in leaf form.

The best-known traditional Moroccan dishes are *tagine*, couscous, *b'stilla* (pie) and kebabs. *Tagine* is, in reality, the name of the earthenware pot or bowl with the cone-shaped top (*tagine*) in which this meat and vegetable stew, usually based on lamb, is made. *B'stilla*, on the other hand, is a much more sophisti-cated dish, both in terms of number of ingredients and the preparation process. Couscous is another delicacy that takes its name from the recipient in which it is made, and which consists of a lower pan in which vegetables and meat are cooked, and a perforated upper pan in which *ta'am*, semolina made from flour, is steam cooked. Lamb, beef or *kefta* (mince) kebabs are always grilled over a charcoal fire.

Olives.

3

Potter's kiln (Safi).

Traditional Moroccan meals comprise three courses: a mild starter, usually salad at lunchtime and soup at dinner; a stronger main course, often couscous or *tagine*; and, finally, delicious cakes and pastries or fruit. We should not that the couscous served at lunchtime is different from that served at dinnertime. At lunch, it contains seven vegetables (potato, tomato, onion, carrot, pumpkin, cabbage and turnip), whilst at dinner, it is known as *tfaya*, it is

Spice market.

made only with chickpeas, raisins, almonds, milk and sugar.

On special occasions, such as family reunions, weddings, baptisms, circumcisions and other religious festivities, three plates are prepared: *b'stilla* (pie), *mechoui* (lamb, roasted over a wood fire) and *tfaya* made with free range chicken. For dessert, fruit of the season: oranges, apples, bananas, strawberries, grapes, etc.

Bread and olives are always at hand at meals and as an accompaniment. The most popular bread in Morocco is known as *jubzs* and is usually home-made. This bread is used to scoop up the meat and vegetables, the diners eating their bread "utensil" each time they use it. The fingers are used to with ancestral delicacy and elegance to eat couscous and salad.

The only drink at meal times is water. Mint tea, practically the national drink, is taken throughout the day. It is served in small glasses, its aromas best appreciated if it is slowly sipped. Mint tea is made according to a strict ritual. According to taste, aromatic herbs such as wormwood or orange flower may be added.

In a Moroccan house, meals take place at a round table, bringing together all members of the family. Breakfast is at around 7 in the morning, lunch at 1 pm and dinner at 8 pm. Meals provide the chance for people to meet and talk, building relations with family and friends alike, providing a source of happiness and pleasure in Moroccan homes throughout the country.

MINT TEA

Difficulty: ✳

Preparation time: 15 min

Ingredients for 6 people:

1 teaspoonful green tea

10-15 sugar lumps

The leaves from 1 sprig fresh mint, washed and drained

Hot water

PREPARATION

Pour tea into teapot, add one glass hot water, stir and pour off water.
Add sugar and fill teapot with boiling water. Simmer for 3 or 4 minutes.
Turn off heat, place fresh mint in teapot, stir with a spoon and allow to rest for a few minutes before serving.

Ingredients for 8 people:

Three-layer filling:

Chicken filling:

2 chickens, weighing around 1 kg each, cleaned and quartered
50 g butter
3 kg onions
1 level spoonful salt
1 teaspoonful ground pepper
5 sprigs natural saffron and a pinch of artificial colouring

3 pinches of cinnamon
1 teaspoonful powdered cinnamon
1 chicken stock cube
1 sprig parsley and coriander in equal parts
14 b'stilla pastry leaves

Egg filling:

15 eggs

Almond filling:

750 g almonds

cooking oil
200 g powdered sugar
1 teaspoonful ground cinnamon

To prepare the dish:

1 egg
1 tablespoonful flour
100 g butter

Decoration:

150 g castor sugar
1 teaspoonful ground cinnamon

Bastela (Pastilla) de Poulet

Chicken b'stilla pie

Difficulty: ★★★

Preparation time: 1h 45 min

PREPARATION

Chicken filling:

In a pan, lightly fry the chicken pieces in butter. Add the chicken stock cube, two diced onions, half the coriander, half the sprig of parsley and the spices, except for the powdered cinnamon. Cover with water and simmer until the chicken is tender. Remove chicken from pan, add the rest of the diced onions and the sprig of parsley and simmer.

When the onions are cooked, add the chicken, skinned and boned and diced into cubes around 3 cm in size. Add the powdered cinnamon.

Stir well. Strain and put the sauce aside ready to make the egg filling.

Egg filling:

Beat the 15 eggs in a bowl. Pour all the eggs into the sauce you put aside and stir gently until the mixture solidifies.

Almond filling:

Place 750 g almonds, boiled and peeled, in a frying pan. Cover with oil and lightly fry. When the almonds turn golden, remove from heat and dry with a clean cloth. Finally, grind in mortar mix with sugar and cinnamon.

Preparing the dish:

Beat an egg with flour and put the mixture aside ready to brush the b'stilla pastry leaves. Melt butter in pan and put by. In an ovenproof pan, place a leaf of b'stilla pastry as the base. Create a flower by placing five more leaves around the diameter.

Spread the almond filling in a 40 cm circle. Cover this filling with b'stilla pastry. Place the egg and chicken fillings over this layer. Cover with the remaining five pastry leaves from the centre outwards, folding the leaves under as if making a bed.

Spread butter over the b'stilla. Bake in oven for ten minutes at 100° and grill for a further ten minutes.

Sprinkle with castor sugar and decorate with a little powdered cinnamon.

Bastela (Pastilla) aux Fruits de Mer

Seafood b'stilla (pie)

PREPARATION

In a frying pan, sauté in oil the hake and the peeled prawns. In a saucepan, boil 25 cl water. Add the squid, the pepper and the laurel. Boil for 10 minutes. Drain the squid, remove the laurel and put aside the cooking water.

In a mortar, crush the pepper, the garlic, the crushed herbs and the spices. Dilute with the water from cooking the squid. Stir the hake, the peeled prawns, the squid and the contents of the mortar with the Chinese noodles, soaked, drained and cut into 5 cm strips. Beat the egg with the flour and put aside to paste the b'stilla pastry leaves.

Grease an oven tray with butter and place on b'stilla leaf to serve as the base. Place another five folded leaves on top to form a flower covering one-third of the diameter. Add the filling, the form a 40 cm circle, and cover with another leaf. Surround the filling with the first five leaves placed in the form of a flower, then cover with another five leaves. Then, as if making a bed, fold surplus pastry under the b'stilla. Spread the b'stilla with butter and decorate with the 24 peeled prawns.

Bake for 10 minutes at 180° and 10 minutes under the grill.

Serve hot, decorated with slices of lemon and sprigs of parsley.

Difficulty: ✳✳✳

Preparation time: 2 h

Ingredients for 6 people:

500 g hake fillet, diced into 3 cm portions

500 g small squid, cut into rings

1 kg fresh prawns, peeled

24 prawns, unpeeled

250 g Chinese noodles

1 small cup cooking oil

8 cloves garlic

2 red peppers

1 tablespoonful salt

1 teaspoonful ground pepper

1 tablespoonful ground sweet paprika

1/2 teaspoonful ground hot paprika

Pinch of artificial colouring

1 tablespoonful crushed coriander

1 fish stock cube

4 tablespoons chopped parsley

3 laurel leaves

12 b'stilla pastry leaves

150 g butter

1 tablespoonful flour

1 egg

1 lemon

Lahrira Fassia Classique

Classical Lahrira Fassia

Difficulty: ✱✱✱

Preparation time: 1 h 20 min

Ingredients for 6 people:

250 g beef fillet, diced in 2 cm pieces
100 g rice
250 g chickpeas, soaked
1 tablespoonful tomato purée
1 tablespoonful salt
3 tablespoons fresh coriander, crushed
1/2 teaspoonful ground pepper
Pinch of artificial colouring
1 beef stock cube
2 tablespoons chopped parsley
2 celery leaves, chopped
5 g butter or one tablespoonful Smen sheep's milk butter
1 medium onion
5 medium-sized tomatoes
2 bunches celery, chopped
1 litre water
150 g flour

PREPARATION

In a pressure cooker, sauté the diced meat in butter. Add the diced onion, the chickpeas, the salt and the spices, one of the three spoonfuls of coriander and the celery. Stir well and add one litre of water.

Boil on a high gas until the cooker starts to whistle. Then lower the heat and boil for 45 minutes. Meanwhile, dilute the flour in a large glass of water.

Liquidise the tomatoes, a glass of water and the diluted flour.

Put this preparation through the blender, then pour into a saucepan and boil. Add the beef stock cube, the rice, the tomato purée, diluted in a glass of water, two spoonfuls of coriander and two spoonfuls of parsley. Simmer until the rice is cooked.

In the pressure cooker, ensure that the chickpeas are cooked and add contents to saucepan.

Boil for 10 minutes. Salt and pepper to taste if necessary.

Serve hot in mugs. Accompany with lemon quarters, dates, dried figs and gri-wechs (small Moroccan cakes made with honey).

Le Méchoui d'Agneau
Lamb méchoui

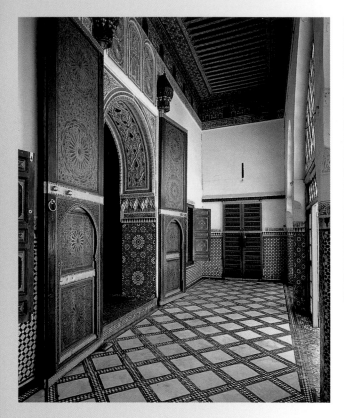

Difficulty: ✳✳✳

Preparation time: 5 h

Ingredients for 12 people:

Half a 10 kg lamb
250 g butter
100 g green olives, stoned
50 g gherkins
200 g red cheese
4 spoonfuls cumin
4 teaspoonfuls salt
2 lettuces

Marrakech: Bahia Palace.

PREPARATION

Melt the butter. Place the meat, uncut, into a large baking pan. Cover it with the melted butter and place in the oven, mark 6 (200°). Bake for around five hours.
Baste with the butter from time to time until the meat is cooked.

Serving:
Cover the bottom of the tray with the dry lettuce leaves. Place the meat on top. Decorate with green olives, gherkin and diced red cheese.
Serve salt and cumin separately, as in the photograph.

Eat hot with mint tea.

Viande d'Agneau aux Amandes et aux Œufs - « Tfaia »

Tfaia (lamb with almonds and eggs)

Difficulty: ✷✷

Preparation time: 1 h 20 min

Ingredients for 6 or 8 people:

1,6 kg meat (preferably shoulder of lamb)

6 medium-sized red onions, diced

450 g quality almonds

4 hard-boiled eggs

1 small sprig coriander

1 teaspoonful ginger

1/2 tablespoonful pepper

1 teaspoonful salt

1 pinch artificial colouring

12 strands natural saffron

1/2 teacup oil

1 teaspoonful sheep's milk butter (Smen) or 1/2 teacup melted butter

PREPARATION

Place spices and oil in a salad bowl and mix well.

Dip pieces of meat one by one into this mixture and leave to marinate for 25 minutes.

Place meat in pressure cooker on top of onions and add sheep's milk butter and coriander.

Lightly fry on a low heat, stirring all the time, for 5 or 10 minutes.

Cover with water, bring to the boil. When the cooker begins to whistle, lower heat and simmer for 45 minutes.

Meanwhile, place almonds, boiled and peeled, in a frying pan, cover with all and fry gently until golden.

Remove once golden, and dry on kitchen roll.

Once cooked, remove meat from cooker and bake in oven until golden (180°).

Meanwhile, reduce sauce in pressure cooker. To serve, arrange the hot pieces of meat in a dish, cover with sauce, scatter almonds on top and decorate with hard-boiled eggs, cut in half.

Serve with mint tea.

Rabat: Hassan tower.

15

Lmhammar de Mouton
Lamb Lmhammar

Difficulty: ✱✱

Preparation time: 1 h 5 min

Ingredients for 6 people:

1,5 kg lamb: neck and shoulder

2 large onions, diced

5 cloves garlic

1 tablespoonful sweet paprika

1 beef stock cube

A little salt

Pinch of artificial colouring

12 strands saffron

1 teaspoonful butter preferably salted (Smen),

or 50 g unsalted butter

1/2 small cup cooking oil

One sprig coriander

Marrakech: Jamaa Lfna square.

PREPARATION

Wash the meat, cut into pieces and strain. In a pressure cooker, gently fry the onions in oil for around 5 minutes.
Meanwhile, crush the garlic and the spices in the mortar. Spread this mixture over the pieces of meat with and place in the pan with the onions. Add the salted butter (*Smen*) and the beef stock cube.

Cook for 2 or 3 minutes, then cover with water. Close the cooker and boil for 45 minutes.
Check that the meat is cooked. Remove meat from cooker and place in a baking pan. Bake for around 10 minutes until golden and reduce the sauce.
To serve, arrange the pieces of meat on as round plate and cover with the sauce, having removed the fat.
Serve hot with mint tea.

Tagine de Mrozia
Mrozia tagine

Difficulty: ✷✷

Preparation time: 1 h 20 min

Casablanca: Hassan II Mosque.

Ingredients for 6 people:

1,5 kg leg of lamb
700 g red raisins (with or sin seeds)
200 g almonds
1 large onion
1 tablespoonful Ras el hanout*
1 teaspoonful ginger
1/2 spoonful artificial colouring
12 strands natural saffron
5 cloves garlic, crushed
1 teaspoonful cinnamon
200 g honey
1/2 small cup olive oil

* Ras el hanout: blend of dried spices (enquire with your local herbalist).

PREPARATION

Sauté the diced onion in a pan with the oil. Place the pieces of meat, clean and dry, in the pan. Add the garlic and all the spices except the cinnamon.
Simmer for 5 minutes.
Cover with water, close the pan and boil for around 50 minutes, checking that there is enough water from time to time. Add water if necessary.
Wash and dry the raisins thoroughly.

Add the raisins to the meat and simmer for around 10 minutes.
Pour in the honey, sprinkle with cinnamon and reduce sauce before turning off heat.
Place the almonds, boiled and peeled, in a frying pan. Cover with oil and gently fry. Remove the almonds from the frying pan when golden and dry with kitchen roll.
Finally, serve the pieces of meat on a round plate and cover with the raisin sauce. Decorate with the almonds. Serve hot, accompanied by mint tea.

Tagine de Veau aux Pruneaux

Tagine of Veal with prunes

PREPARATION

In a pressure cooker, lightly fry the meat portions in oil. Add the crushed garlic, one quarter of the diced onions, the beef stock cube, the ginger, the salt and the two strands of saffron. Cover with water and boil on a high gas until the pressure cooker starts to whistle. Then lower the heat and simmer until the meat is cooked.

Remove the meat when cooked. Put two saucepans of stock by to cook the prunes. Add the remaining sliced onions. Simmer until the onions are tender. Reduce the stock if necessary.

In another pan, place the stock put aside from cooking. Add salt and pepper and the washed prunes. Simmer until tender and add, in this order, the sugar, the cinnamon and the honey.

In a frying pan, sauté the almonds, boiled and peeled. Remove from oil and dry.

In another frying pan, gently fry the sesame grains without oil.

Place olive oil in a saucepan and add the meat. Heat to boiling point just before serving.

In a 40 cm diameter plate, place the portions de meat and, on top, the onions and the sauce. Decorate with prunes fried in sesame and the almonds.

Difficulty: ✷✷

Preparation time: 1 h 15 min

Ingredients for 6 people:

For the meat:

1,5 kg shoulder of veal, cut into six portions

1 small cup cooking oil

1/2 small cup olive oil

1 kg onions

4 cloves garlic

1 tablespoonful salt

1 teaspoonful powdered ginger

5 strands natural saffron

1 pinch of artificial colouring

1 beef stock cube

For the prunes:

1 tablespoonful powdered cinnamon

1 kg dried prunes

150 g powdered sugar

1/2 small cup honey

For the decoration:

200 g almonds

100 g sesame grains

Tagine Berbère aux Sept Légumes

Berber Tagine with seven vegetables

Difficulty: ✳✳

Preparation time: 1 h 40 min

Ingredients for 8 people:

1,5 kg shoulder of veal
1/2 teaspoonful pepper
1 teaspoonful salt
Pinch of artificial colouring
1 small cup cooking oil
1/2 small cup olive oil
1 beef stock cube
2 large onions
6 cloves garlic
1 carrot
1 courgette
1 potato
1 tomato
3 peppers (red, yellow and green)
150 g peas
1 turnip
2 tablespoons chopped parsley

PREPARATION

In a pan, lightly fry the meat with the oil, the pepper, the salt, the saffron, a diced onion and the crushed garlic. Cover with water and boil for 15 minutes.

Place the preparation in a shallow *tagine*, arrange the vegetables, cut in half or quartered, the peppers, sliced into 1 cm thick strips, the onions, sliced, the beef stock and parsley. Cover with water.

Simmer until the meat the vegetables are good and tender. Add water if needed.

Add the olive oil at the last minute.

Serve hot.

Berber girl.

Tagine d'Agneau aux fonds d'Artichauts

Lamb tagine with artichoke hearts

PREPARATION

Lightly fry the meat with oil in a pan. Add the spices and stir for around 10 minutes. Add the onions and lightly fry.
Cover with water and add half of the beef stock cube.
Simmer. Add water if necessary.
Put aside the meat.
Put a little stock from cooking the meat into another pan. Add a little salt, the colouring, a little pepper and the other half of the stock cube.
When boiling, add the rice, well washed. Cover with water and simmer. Add water if necessary. The rice should absorb all the stock.
In the remaining stock, cook the artichoke hearts with the crystallised lemon. Add a little water if necessary (the stock should be thick).
Before removing from heat, place the meat in the pan with the small cup olive oil.
Place the rice in a large cup in the centre of a round plate. Arrange the meat and the artichokes around it, with the sauce.

Difficulty: ✶✶

Preparation time: 1 h 15 min

Ingredients for 6 people:

1 kg lamb, cut into 6 pieces
250 g onions, diced
4 cloves garlic
1 teaspoonful ginger
1/2 teaspoonful salt
1/2 teaspoonful pepper
Pinch of artificial colouring
1/2 small cup cooking oil
1/2 small cup olive oil
12 artichoke hearts, cleaned and sprinkled with lemon juice
200 g rice
1 beef stock cube
2 large glasses water
1/2 crystallised lemon
1 cup green olives

Meknes: the Bab el Mansour gate.

Tagine de Veau aux Olives Concassées

Beef tagine with ground olives

Difficulty: ✹✹

Preparation time: 1 h 15 min

Souk Oued Laou (Tangier Region).

Ingredients for 8 people:

1,5 kg beef heel of round, cut into pieces

500 g olives, stoned

2 medium-sized onions, diced

1 large tomato, grated

8 cloves garlic, crushed

1 small cup cooking oil

1/2 small cup olive oil

1 teaspoonful ginger

Pinch of artificial colouring

1 teaspoonful salt

1 beef stock cube

2 tablespoons chopped parsley

2 tablespoons fresh coriander, crushed

PREPARATION

In a frying pan, sauté the meat with the colouring, the salt, ginger, the oil, the onions, the garlic and the beef stock for between 5 and 10 minutes. Cover with water and simmer until half cooked.

In a pan, boil one litre of water with a quarter of lemon. Soak the olives for 10 minutes to remove the salt. Remove from water and add to the preparation with the tomato, the coriander and the parsley.

Finish cooking, always checking that there is enough water, adding more if necessary. Finally, add the olive oil. Serve hot.

27

Tagine de Veau aux Choux de Bruxelles et aux Carottes

Beef tagine with Brussels sprouts and carrots

Difficulty: ✳

Preparation time: 1 h

Traditional oven made from clay mixed with straw.

Ingredients for 6 or 8 people:

1,6 kg shoulder of beef, in pieces
1/2 kg medium-sized carrots, washed
1/2 kg Brussels sprouts, well washed in salty water
6 cloves garlic (preferably red)
1 small onion, finely diced
1/2 small glass oil

1/2 small glass olive oil
1 teaspoonful ginger
1 teaspoonful salt
1 meat stock cube
1 pinch artificial colouring
1 small sprig coriander

PREPARATION

In a pressure cooker, fry the pieces of meat, washed and drained, in oil until golden, with the garlic, grated, the salt, the ginger and the saffron. Simmer all ingredients together for 5-10 minutes, stirring all the time. Add onions and coriander.

Cover with water and simmer for 40 minutes. When the pressure cooker whistles, lower heat.
Once cooked, remove meat and replace with vegetables until these are also cooked. Add stock cube, crumbled.
Fine minutes before the end, return meat to cooker and sprinkle with olive oil.

Tagine de Veau aux Haricots Verts

Beef tagine with green beans

Difficulty: ✳✳

Preparation time: 1 h 30 min

PREPARATION

Arrange pieces of meat, washed, in a pressure cooker. Add cloves garlic, grated, and the spices (ginger, saffron, salt). Pour on oil and fry lightly for 4 or 5 minutes. Add the tomato and the onion, diced.

Cover with water and bring to boil. When the cooker begins to whistle, lower heat and simmer for 45 minutes.

Meanwhile, steam cook the green beans, washed and cut into 3-cm slices.

Now melt butter in a pan, add the 3 onions, sliced, crumble the stock cube and fry gently until golden for 8 or 10 minutes, stirring with a wooden spoon. To this mixture add the beans, cooked, the pepper, sprinkle a tablespoonful of parsley on top and leave to marinate over a low heat for 5 minutes. Add salt to taste.

Once the meat is cooked, add the rest of the parsley and coriander and lightly fry for 3 minutes. If necessary, reduce the sauce.

To serve, arrange the meat pieces on a round plate, pour sauce over meat and decorate with green beans. Serve hot.

Ingredients for 6 or 8 people:

1,6 kg heel of beef
1 kg green beans
1 large onion, diced
3 medium-sized onions, sliced
6 cloves garlic
1 tomato, peeled, seeded and diced
2 tablespoonfuls parsley, finely chopped
2 tablespoonfuls coriander, finely chopped
1 teaspoonful ginger
1/2 teaspoonful pepper
1 pinch artificial colouring
1 teaspoonful salt
1 meat stock cube
1/2 small glass oil
1/2 small glass olive oil
1 tablespoonful butter

Marrakech: Water sellers.

Tagine de Veau aux Navets - « Mahfour »

Mahfour (beef tagine with turnips)

Ingredients for 6 or 8 people:

1,5 kg shoulder of beef, cut into pieces

1,5 kg turnips

1 large onion

1/2 teaspoonful pepper

1 pinch artificial colouring

50 g sheep's milk butter (Smen)

2 slices cinnamon

1 teaspoonful salt

1/2 small glass olive oil

1 meat stock cube

2 tablespoonfuls coriander, finely chopped

Moulay Idriss Zerhoun: panoramic view.

Difficulty: ✳

Preparation time: 1 h 5 min

PREPARATION

Place the meat pieces, washed, in a pan. Finely dice onions. Add spices (pepper, saffron, salt, cinnamon, half the stock cube, butter). Mix well and leave to marinate for 5 or 6 minutes.

Cover with water, place lid on top and simmer for around 45 minutes. Check from time to time and add water if necessary.

Meanwhile, peel turnips, dice and put by. Once the meat is cooked, remove from pan, place turnips in pan and simmer with the other ingredients for 12-15 minutes.

Fine minutes before the end, return meat to pan and sprinkle with olive oil and coriander.

If necessary, continue cooking to reduce sauce.

Serve hot.

Tagine de Veaux aux Coings et aux Gombos

Beef tagine with quince and okra

Difficulty: ✹✹

Preparation time: 1 h 30 min

Ingredients for 8 people:

2 kg beef (preferably heel)
1 kg quince
250 g okra (a green pepper spice)
8 large onions
6 cloves garlic
1/2 fresh lemon
1 teaspoonful ginger
1/2 teaspoonful pepper
Pinch of artificial colouring
1 teaspoonful salt
1/2 small cup cooking oil
1/2 small cup olive oil
1 beef stock cube

PREPARATION

In a pressure cooker, sauté two peeled and sliced onions.

Place the pieces of meat, previously washed, in the cooker.
Crush the garlic.
Add ginger, colouring, salt and the oil.
Simmer for around 5 minutes.
Cover with water and cook for 40 minutes.

Meanwhile:
Cut the quinces in quarters, scoop out fruit and wash. Boil in a pan with the half lemon.
Peel and slice the rest of the onions. Wash and dry well.
Once the meat is cooked, put it aside and keep it hot.
Put aside a pan of beef stock to cook the okra.
Add the onions and half of the beef stock cube and cook for around 10 minutes.
Add the quince, cut into quarters and well drained. Add the olive oil. Cover and boil for about 10 minutes, reducing the stock if necessary.
Wash the okra and remove the stalks. Place them in a pan with the beef stock put aside. Add the half of the stock cube and the pepper. Cover with water and simmer for 15 minutes.

Serve as in the photograph.

Medfouna à la Viande

Medfouna with meat

Difficulty: ✷✷

Preparation time: 1 h 45 min

Rissani.

Ingredients for 8 people:

<u>Dough :</u>

500 g durum flour

1 spoonful baker's yeast

1/2 teaspoonful salt

A little water to make the dough

<u>Filling:</u>

1 kg ox fillet, diced

1 large onion, grated

1 small cup parsley, finely chopped

2 tablespoons crushed coriander grains

1 teaspoonful pepper

1 teaspoonful salt

1/2 teaspoonful cumin

1/2 teaspoonful cinnamon

1/2 small cup cooking oil

Bread base:

Stir the ingredients for the dough. Knead, divide into two balls and leave half an hour to ferment.

Filling:

Heat the oven. Stir all the ingredients described for the filling and leave to ferment for half an hour.

On the kitchen table, roll one ball of dough into a 1/2 cm thick strip. Place in a 40 cm diameter baking pan. Prick dough with a fork. Pour on filling and cover with the other ball of dough, similarly rolled. Paste the edges and round. Prick with fork. Place in the oven (150°) for around 45 minutes. Serve Medfouna hot accompanied by a glass of mint tea. According to taste, this dish can also be accompanied by a spicy sauce.

Brochettes de Veau
Beef kebabs

Difficulty: ✷

Preparation time: 1 h

Ingredients for 6 people:

1,5 kg beef fillet

2 large onions, finely sliced

1/2 teaspoonful white pepper

1/2 teaspoonful black pepper

1/2 teaspoonful cinnamon

1 teaspoonful cumin

2 tablespoons cooking oil

6 tablespoons chopped parsley

1 teaspoonful salt (to taste)

Erfoud.

PREPARATION

Wash and drain the meat.
Dice the meat.
Add the onion, parsley, cumin and cinnamon. Add salt and pepper to taste. Pour on two tablespoons oil and stir. Leave to marinate for one hour.
Place 6 pieces of meat on each kebab skewer and grill over charcoal or on the barbeque.
Serve with mint tea.

Tagine de Kabab Maghdour

Maghdour Tagine Kebabs

Kebabs are skewers of meat, either carbon grilled or made in tagine dishes, known as Kabab Maghdour.

Difficulty: ✳

Preparation time: 1 h

PREPARATION

In a saucepan, lightly fry the meat with the saffron, the oil, the rancid butter, the beef stock, the salt and the spices. Add the onions, the garlic, the coriander and, finally, the tomatoes. Cover with water and cook until the meat is tender. Check the level of the stock and add water if necessary.
Remove the meat from the pan and reduce the stock. Reheat everything.
Fry the eggs and place them on the meat. This dish can also be made without the eggs. Serve hot with mint tea.

Ingredients for 8 people:

1,5 kg leg of veal, boned and diced
1 kg onions, finely sliced
8 cloves garlic, crushed
1 tablespoonful rancid butter
1 small cup cooking oil
1 pinch of industrial colouring
1 spoonful paprika
1/2 teaspoonful pepper
1 teaspoonful salt
2 tomatoes, grated
1 beef stock cube
1 tablespoonful fresh coriander, crushed
8 eggs

Fes: overall view.

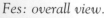

40

Ingredients for 6 people:

10 kg leg of veal, boned	3 kg grease
1/2 kg coriander grains	4 l de olive oil
400 g garlic	3 l cooking oil
500 g salt	1 50 cl bottle of vinegar
100 g cumin	1 teaspoonful thyme
100 g ground caraway seed	1 tablespoonful whole caraway seed

Khlii

MEAT

Khlii is dried meat, covered with vegetable fat and olive oil in a way which allowed our grandparents to conserve it throughout the year in earthenware jars.

To prepare the meat:

Cut the meat into strips 50 cm long and 4 cm thick. Wash the meat and allow to drain.

Crush the garlic, unpeeled, and the salt in a mortar.

In a large bowl, place the sliced coriander, cumin and the ground caraway seeds. Add the garlic and the salt. Stir well (marinade).

Place the meat in a plastic recipient. Sprinkle with the marinade. Add the vinegar and 2 small cups of olive oil. Stir well to ensure that all the meat absorbs the marinade. Cover with a cloth and leave to marinate for 24 hours.

On the afternoon of the following day, stretch out the pieces of meat, ensuring that they do not touch each other. Dry meat completely (minimum six days in summer).

To cook:

Place the thyme and the caraway seeds in a small, fine, white bag or bouquet. Wash the fresh fat. Drain and mince.

In a large saucepan, boil 4 litres of water. Add the minced fat, the cooking oil and the olive oil. Boil for 10 to 15 minutes. Soak

Difficulty: ✹✹✹

Preparation time: 5-6 h

the pieces of meat and the bouquet of herbs in this stock.

Leave uncovered and boil, stirring with a wooden spoon from time to time to ensure that the meat does not become stuck to the bottom of the pan. Boil for around five hours.

Turn off the gas. Remove the white froth using a fine colander. Fill clean recipients half-full with the fat (khlii lidam).

Remove all the pieces of meat. Allow to drain and cool in a colander. Don't forget to remove the bouquet of herbs.

To make the *agriche*, simmer until the sauce has been completed reduced. Allow to cool and put aside in a clean recipient. Place the pieces of meat in the recipients containing the fat (lidam). Do not cover the recipients. Allow to rest for 12 hours.

You can serve this dish with free range eggs. Delicious with mint tea.

43

Tagine de Kadide (Viande Condée) aux Tomates

Kadide (mince) tagine with tomatoes

Difficulty: ✳

Preparation time: 1 h

Tangier.

Ingredients for 6 people:

1/2 kg kadide (mince), chopped
1,5 kg tomatoes, peeled and diced
4 cloves garlic
1/2 teaspoonful ground coriander grains
2 tablespoons chopped parsley
1/2 cup cooking oil

1/2 cup olive oil
Pinch of artificial colouring
1 teaspoonful paprika
1/2 teaspoonful pepper
1 hot red pepper

PREPARATION

In a large saucepan, boil the tomatoes with the oil, the crushed garlic, the spices and the coriander.

Add the meat and boil for 45 minutes, until the sauce has been reduced, then add the parsley and the olive oil. Serve hot with mint tea.

Tanjia Marrakchia de Veau

Veal Tanjia Marrakchia

Difficulty: ✱✱✱

Preparation time: 2 h

Ingredients for 8 people:

2 kg leg of veal with bone, cut into pieces
1 small cup cooking oil
2 tomatoes, peeled and grated
2 large onions
8 cloves garlic
1 tablespoonful salt
1 teaspoonful ground pepper
1 tablespoonful sweet paprika
1 teaspoonful powdered ginger
10 strands natural saffron
Pinch of artificial colouring
1 tablespoonful ground grain coriander
1 beef stock cube

Just before serving:

1/2 small cup olive oil
1 tablespoonful powdered cumin
2 tablespoons vinegar

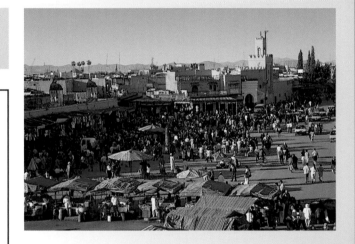

Marrakech: Jamaa Lfna square.

PREPARATION

The *tanjia* is an oven-baked earthenware recipient varnished on the inside. Once filled with the dish described here, it is covered with kraft paper and left amongst embers all night. A pressure cooker can, however, be used instead of the *tanjia*.

In a pressure cooker, lightly fry the pieces of meat in oil. Add the grated tomatoes, the onions, diced, the salt, the pepper, the paprika, ginger, the saffron, the colouring, the ground coriander grains and the beef stock cube. Cover with water and boil at a high gas until the cooker begins to whistle. Then lower gas and bake until the meat is tender. Remove the pieces of meat and reduce the stock if necessary, before placing the meat in the cooker once more. Add the olive oil, powdered cumin and vinegar and simmer.

Serve very hot on a 40 cm diameter round plate.

Couscous Makhzani aux Sept Légumes

"Makhzani" couscous with seven vegetables

Marrakech. Palacio Bahia.

Difficulty: ✳✳✳

Preparation time: 2 h

Pour couscous into a bowl. Wet with 150 cl water. Allow to rest for 5 minutes and knead gently with both hands. Place couscous in the upper couscous pan. Join the two pans and steam for 20 minutes. Repeat the same process once more.

Remove the upper couscous pan to check whether meat is cooked. When cooked, put it aside and place the vegetables and the sprig of herbs in the pan.

Repeat the process with the grain a third time.

Remove lid from upper pan. Pour the couscous into a bowl. Add the other half of the butter and stir gently to air, using wooden spatula. Gently cook the vegetables in the lower couscous pan at low heat. In a 40 cm diameter round plate, make a cone with the couscous. Place the meat on top and in the centre, decorate with the vegetables and cover with the sauce. Do not use much sauce at first –you can always add more. Serve hot, as in the photograph.

PREPARATION

In the lower couscous pan, lightly fry the meat, cut into small pieces, and two finely sliced onions in the oil and half the butter. Add the chickpeas, the herbs, the spices and the beef stock cube, dissolved in a little water. Cover with water and simmer.

Ingredients for 8 people:

1 kg meat (shoulder of veal)

1 kg medium wheat semolina (couscous)

250 g chickpeas, soaked overnight in water

6 courgettes, sliced in half down the middle

6 small turnips, sliced in half down the middle

12 small carrots sliced in half down the middle

6 small potatoes, cut into quarters

1 cabbage, cut into twelve pieces

1 slice of pumpkin, cut into six long pieces

6 medium-sized onions

4 tomatoes: two cut into quarters, two crushed

1 spicy green pepper

100 g butter

1 small cup cooking oil

1 spoonful salt

1/2 teaspoonful ground pepper

Pinch of artificial colouring

1 beef stock cube

1 sprig, made up of one part parsley and two parts coriander

Couscous Tfaya aux Raisins et Amandes

"Tfaya" couscous with raisins and almonds

Difficulty: ✱✱✱

Preparation time: 2 h

Ingredients for 8 people:

1 kg meat (shoulder of veal)
1 kg medium wheat semolina
250 g chickpeas, soaked
1 small cup cooking oil
100 g butter
2 kg onions
1/2 teaspoonful ground pepper
1 tablespoonful salt
1 beef stock cube
1 sprig coriander
500 g seedless raisins
150 g powdered sugar
1 teaspoonful powdered cinnamon
Pinch of artificial colouring
500 g almonds

PREPARATION

In the lower couscous pan, lightly fry the meat, cut into small pieces, and two finely sliced onions in the oil and half the butter. Add the chickpeas, the herbs, the beef stock and the spices, except for the sugar and cinnamon. Cover with water and simmer.

When cooked, remove the pieces of meat and add two thirds of the onions, roughly chopped, to the stock. Simmer until the onions are tender.

In another pan, pour a little of the stock, add the other third of the roughly chopped onions and the raisins. Add salt and pepper to taste. Simmer until the onions are tender and add the sugar and cinnamon. Simmer.

In a frying pan, gently fry the almonds, boiled and peeled, in oil. When golden, remove from frying pan and dry.

Place couscous in a bowl and wet with 150 cl water. Allow to rest for 5 minutes and knead gently with both hands. Place couscous in the upper couscous pan and this pan over boiling pan. Cook for 20 minutes. Repeat the same process a second time. Remove the upper couscous pan to check whether meat is cooked. When cooked, remove and add the vegetables and the herbs.

Repeat the process a third time. Remove the upper couscous pan and pour couscous into a bowl. Add the other half of the butter and stir gently with a wooden spatula. Simmer lower pan gently.

In a 40 cm diameter round plate, make a cone with the couscous. Place the meat on top and cover with a little sauce at first —you can always add more later. Decorate with a teaspoonful of powdered cinnamon. Serve hot, as in the photograph.

Brkoukss (Couscous Soussi)

Brkoukss (Soussi couscous)

Agadir: overall view.

Difficulty: ✳✳

Preparation time: 1 h 15 min

Ingredients for 8 people:

1 kg couscous
50 g butter
1 tablespoonful salt
1/2 small cup cooking oil
1 large cup Amlou
Argan oil
2 litres milk serum

PREPARATION

Boil water en the lower couscous pan.

Place couscous on a soup plate. Add the salt and the oil. Sprinkle with 150 cl water. Knead the couscous with both hands to remove any lumps and allow to rest for 2 or 3 minutes. Gradually pour couscous into the upper pan and steam for around 20 minutes.

Remove lid from upper couscous pan. Pour couscous onto a soup plate, sprinkle with water and stir down-up with a wooden spoon.

Check water level in the pan and place couscous to cook once more.

After 20 minutes, repeat the operation a third time.

When cooked, place couscous in a deep salad bowl and add butter.

Serve on a round plate with the Amlou in the centre.

Accompany with Argan oil and milk serum.

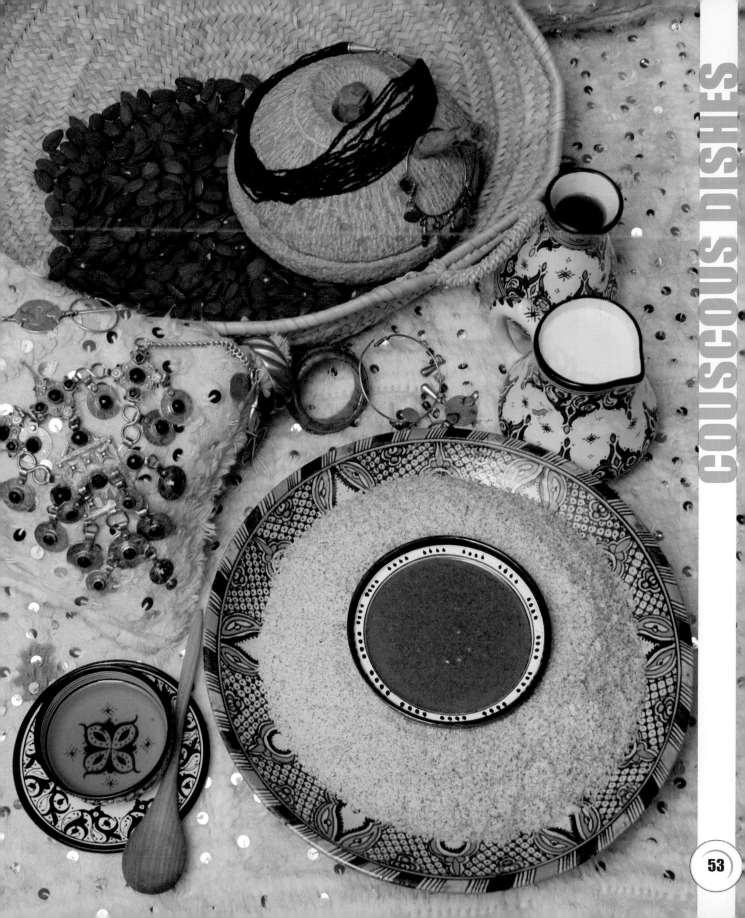

Couscous Soussi
Soussi couscous

Difficulty: ✳✳✳

Preparation time: 2 h

Ingredients for 8 people:

1,5 kg beef or veal

1 kg medium wheat semolina

5 medium-sized onions

4 courgettes cut in half

4 carrots, cut in half

4 turnips, cut in half

2 tomatoes, grated

400 g pumpkin, cut into eight pieces

100 g butter

Sprig of parsley and coriander

1 beef stock cube

1 small cup cooking oil

1 tablespoonful salt

Pinch of industrial colouring

1 teaspoonful pepper

1 teaspoonful powdered thyme

1 large cup Amlou

1 large cup Argan oil

2 litres milk serum

PREPARATION

Place two sliced onions, half the oil and butter and the pieces of meat in the lower couscous pan. Add salt and pepper, cover with water and simmer.

Meanwhile, pour couscous into a deep recipient, and sprinkle with 150 cl water and the remaining oil.

Salt and knead the couscous gently with both hands. Gradually pour couscous into the upper pan, seal the couscous pan and simmer.

After half an hour, unfasten the couscous pan and empty the upper pan onto the soup plate. Sprinkle the couscous with water again, and stir down-up with a wooden spoon. Simmer again in the same way. Check that there is still enough water in the lower pan.

Thirty minutes later, repeat the same operation for the third time.

Check to see how the meat is cooking. Put aside when cooked, then add the vegetables, the sprig of parsley and coriander and the stock cube.

When cooked, unfasten the upper couscous pan and pour couscous into a salad bowl before adding butter.

Place couscous in a round bowl and sprinkle with the sauce. Arrange the meat and vegetables around it and sprinkle on more sauce.

Serve dish with a large cup of Amlou, the Argan oil and the milk serum mixed with the powdered thyme.

Tagine de Pieds de Veau (Hergma)

Tagine of hoof of beef (Hergma)

Taroudante.

Difficulty: ✷✷

Preparation time: 1 h 45 min

Ingredients for 8 people:

2 beef hoofs, clean and dry, sliced

2 cups chickpeas, soaked

2 cups rice

1 large onion, diced

6 cloves garlic, crushed

Pinch of artificial colouring

1 large tomato, grated

1 tablespoonful paprika

1/2 teaspoonful ginger

1 teaspoonful salt

1 beef stock cube

1 small cup cooking oil

1/2 small cup olive oil

PREPARATION

Place the calf's hoofs, cut into slices, in a pan with the rest of the ingredients, except for the rice. Cover with water and simmer until the meat is cooked. Check water level regularly, adding more if necessary.

In a pan, place a little stock from boiling the calf's hoofs. Add the rice and a little salt. Cover with water and simmer until the water is completely absorbed.
Serve hot, placing the rice in a bowl in the centre of the dish so that it does not absorb the sauce.

OFFAL

Tagine de Skhina
Skhina Tagine

Difficulty: ✳✳

Preparation: 1 h 45 min

El Jadida:
The Angel Bastion.

PREPARATION

In the pressure cooker, place the pieces of meat and hoof, well washed.

Add the chickpeas, grate the garlic and add, and season with paprika and salt. Pour in one small glass oil. Put the corn into a perforated metal ball, close firmly and place in cooker.

Cover with water and bring to boil.

When the cooker begins to whistle, lower heat and simmer until the meat is well cooked (around 1 and a half hours).

Meanwhile, boil the eggs.

Add potatoes and eggs, peeled, 10 minutes before cooking ends. Serve hot.

Ingredients for 8 people:

1 kg beef shank, cut into slices

2 beef hoofs, cut into 8 pieces

200 g chickpeas, soaked in water overnight

200 g husked corn, soaked in water overnight

4 eggs

4 small potatoes, cut into quarters

6 cloves garlic

1 tablespoonful paprika

1 teaspoonful salt

1 small glass olive oil

Note: this dish can be prepared in the traditional way over carbon on the barbecue, though cooking time will be considerably longer.

Tagine de Foie M'chermel à la Fassie

Fassia M'chermel liver tagine

Difficulty: ✳✳

Preparation time: 1 h

Zagora.

Ingredients for 6 people:

1 kg beef liver, sliced
8 cloves garlic
1 sprig of parsley and coriander, crushed
1 red pepper
2 tablespoons flour
4 tablespoons vinegar
1 teaspoonful pepper
2 teaspoonfuls cumin
1 teaspoonful paprika
1 teaspoonful salt
1 beef stock cube
1 small cup cooking oil
1/2 small cup olive oil
1/2 crystallised lemon and some red olives for decoration

PREPARATION

Prepare the marinade by beating the garlic, parsley, the coriander, the sliced red pepper, the pepper, the paprika, the salt, one teaspoonful of cumin and 2 spoonfuls of vinegar.

Add salt and pepper to the sliced liver and fry with a small cup of oil. Then dice liver. Place the liver in a pan with the marinade. Add a little water, the beef stock cube and the oil from frying the liver. Boil for 15 minutes.

Place the flour in a large cup with a little water. Stir well and pour into the pan. Boil for 5 minutes. Add the olive oil, the vinegar and cumin before removing from heat. Serve hot or cold. Decorate to taste.

Tagine de Merlan Farci
Tagine of stuffed sea trout

Difficulty: ✹✹✹

Preparation time: 1 h 20 min

Ingredients for 6 or 8 people:

2 sea trout, each weighing around 500 g
250 g peeled prawns
250 g squid, cleaned and sliced into rings
8 prawns
200 g Chinese noodles, soaked
2 large tomatoes, grated
2 tomatoes, sliced
2 potatoes, chopped
1 green pepper, sliced
1 red pepper
100 g olives, stoned and sliced
The peel of one candied lemon
1/2 teaspoonful thyme
2 bay leaves
1/2 small glass oil
1/2 small glass olive oil
1 lemon
2 dessertspoonfuls parsley
50 g black olives (10-12 olives)
1 fish stock cube

For the Charmoula (sauce):

1 sprig parsley and coriander, chopped
8 cloves garlic, chopped
1 red pepper, chopped
1 tablespoonful cumin
1 tablespoonful paprika
1 tablespoonful pepper
1 teaspoonful salt
The peel of one candied lemon
1/2 small glass vinegar

PREPARATION

Soak the noodles in cold water for 30 minutes.
Mix together all the ingredients for the Charmoula (sauce).
Spread 1/3 of this mixture over the fish and leave to marinate for 15 minutes.
Place the potatoes at the bottom of a pan and add the second 1/3 of the Charmoula, the chopped tomatoes, the bay leaves and the saffron, crumble the fish stock cube and add oil. Cover with water and simmer for around 15 minutes.
Meanwhile, fry half the prawns in one tablespoonful butter until golden. Season and arrange in a salad bowl.
Add the noodles, drained and chopped, a tablespoonful from the remaining Charmoula, the green olives, sliced and the candied lemon peel, diced; season and mix well.
Stuff the two fish with this mixture.
Arrange the potatoes in a baking dish, place the two stuffed fish over them and decorate with squid rings, tomatoes, peppers, the remaining prawns, the black olives and the lemon.
Pour the remaining Charmoula over the potatoes, adding a small glass of water if necessary. Stir and pour sauce and olive oil over fish.
Sprinkle with thyme and parsley.
Place in oven and bake for 30-40 minutes at 180°.
Fry prawns in butter, parsley, pepper and salt. Decorate the plate with these prawns before serving.

Pageot Farcie aux Fruits de Mer

Sea bream stuffed with seafood

PREPARATION

Soak the rice noodles in water. In a food processor, blend all the ingredients for the marinade and baste the fish with a little of this mixture. Lightly fry half the peeled prawns in the table oil. Season and put by in a bowl. Add the noodles, strained and sliced, 2 soupspoons of the marinade, half the confited lemon peel, salt and pepper.
Stuff the sea bream with this preparation and arrange on an oven dish.
Add a glass of water and the chopped tomatoes to the remaining marinade sauce and spread around the fish. Cover with sliced vegetables, squid, prawns olives and the remaining lemon peel. Sprinkle with thyme.
Sprinkle with olive oil and bake in a pre-heated oven (180°C) for one hour. Add more water if necessary to obtain a creamy sauce.

Sautée the king prawns to decorate the dish. Squeeze lemon juice over the fish and serve in the oven dish.

Difficulty: ✳✳✳

Preparation time: 2 h 30 min

Ingredients for 6 people:

1 sea bream weighing around 3 kilos
250 g peeled prawns
250 g squid, sliced
250 g king prawns
250 g rice noodles, soaked
250 g tomatoes, sliced
250 g tomato, chopped
1 red pimento, sliced
1 green pimento, sliced
Olives
The peel of 1 lemon, confited
½ teaspoon thyme
½ small glass olive oil
½ small glass table oil

For the marinade (charmoula):

1 sprig parsley and coriander, chopped
8 cloves garlic, chopped
1 red pimento, diced
1 tablespoon cumin
1 tablespoon paprika
1 teaspoon pepper
1 teaspoon salt
The peel of half a lemon, confited
½ small glass vinegar

Tagine de Sardines

Sardine tagine

Difficulty: ✱✱

Preparation time: 1 h

Safi: Fishing port
(sardines).

Ingredients for 6 people:

1 kg sardine fillets
250 g tomatoes, grated
250 g tomatoes, sliced
1 green pepper, cut into rings
1 small red pepper
2 lemons
1 large cup green olives
1 small cup olive oil

For the marinade:

1 sprig of parsley and crushed coriander
8 cloves garlic, crushed
1 red pepper, sliced
1 tablespoonful cumin
1 tablespoonful paprika
1 teaspoonful pepper
1 teaspoonful salt
The peel from 1/2 crystallised lemon
1/2 small cup vinegar

PREPARATION

Liquidise all the ingredients for the marinade. Place the sardines to marinate for 1/2 hour in half the marinade.
Add 1/2 glass of water to the rest of the marinade and place in the *tagine* with the grated tomatoes.

Arrange the sliced tomatoes and the green pepper. Arrange the sardine fillets in twos, in a circle. Add the sliced lemon, the olives and the pepper. Sprinkle with olive oil. Bake for about 30 minutes.

Serve with lemon juice.

Tagine de Poulet Beldi M'hammer

M'hammer chicken tagine

PREPARATION

Difficulty: ✷✷

Preparation time: 2 h 30 min

Ingredients for 6 people:

3 chickens, each weighing around 1 kg
1/2 small cup cooking oil
50 g butter or one tablespoonful sheep's milk butter (Smen)
9 cloves garlic
6 medium-sized onions
3 tablespoons salt
1/2 teaspoonful ground pepper
1 tablespoonful sweet paprika
12 strands natural saffron
Pinch of artificial colouring
1 chicken stock cube
1 tablespoonful vinegar
1 teaspoonful ground ginger

Clean the chickens and rub with salt (one tablespoonful per chicken). Place the chickens in a large pan, add the vinegar, cover with water and leave the chickens in the refrigerator to soak overnight.

Crush the garlic and the spices in a mortar and the sheep's milk butter (Smen). Dry the chickens well and spread with the mixture from mortar.

In a large saucepan, place the oil and the butter and sauté the chickens and their livers for 10 minutes. Add the diced onions. Gently fry for another 5 minutes.

Cover with water and simmer for around 90 minutes. Check that there is enough water from time to time, adding more if necessary. Remove the chickens and the livers when cooked. Reduce the sauce, taking the lid off, until all the water has evaporated.

In a large cup, dilute the chicken stock cube in one tablespoonful of butter. Spread the mixture all over the chickens.

Place the chickens in the oven under the grill at

180°. Turn gently from time to time until they become golden, without becoming dry.

Dice the chicken and stir into one tablespoonful of the sauce.

Place the chickens on a 40 cm diameter plate, the necks towards the centre. Sprinkle with the sauce.

Tagine de Poulet Beldi M'qalli

Beldi M'qalli chicken tagine

Difficulty: ✳✳

Preparation time: 2 h 30 min

Ingredients for 6 people:

3 chickens, each weighing around 1 kg
1/2 small cup cooking oil
1/2 small cup olive oil
9 cloves garlic
6 medium-sized onions
1 tablespoons salt
12 strands natural saffron
Pinch of artificial colouring
1 teaspoonful powdered ginger
1 chicken stock cube
100 g pickled pink olives
1 pickled lemon
1 tablespoonful vinegar

PREPARATION

Wash the chickens and rub with salt (one table-spoonful per chicken).

Place the chickens in a large pan, add the vine-gar and cover with water. Soak chickens in fridge overnight.

In a mortar crush a quarter of the lemon peel, the garlic and the spices. Drain the chickens well and rub skin with the mixture from the mortar.

Place cooking oil and olive oil in a pan and sauté the chickens and chicken livers on either side for 10 minutes. Add the diced onions. Lightly fry for another 5 minutes.

Cover with water and simmer for 90 minutes. Check cooking and water level, adding more if necessary.

Once they are cooked, remove the chickens and the livers. Take lid off pan to reduce the sauce until all the water has evaporated.

Cut lemon peel into 1 cm strips.

Dice the chicken livers and mix with one spoon-ful sauce.

Place the chickens on a 40 cm diameter plate, the necks towards the centre. Sprinkle with the sauce and decorate with the olives and the strips of lemon peel covered by the chicken liver.

Tetouan: Mèchouar square.

Tagine de Poulet aux Carottes

Chicken tagine with carrots

Difficulty: ✳

Preparation time: 1 h

Larache.

Ingredients for 6 people:

1 free range chicken
1,5 kg small carrots, peeled and sliced
250 g onions, diced
5 cloves garlic
1 teaspoonful ginger
1/2 teaspoonful pepper
1 teaspoonful salt

Pinch of artificial colouring
1 small cup cooking oil
1/2 small cup olive oil
1/2 crystallised lemon
2 tablespoons chopped parsley
1 chicken stock cube
1 large cup red olives

PREPARATION

In a pan, sauté the chicken with the spices and the oil for 10 minutes. Add the onions and gently fry. Cover with water and simmer until the meat is cooked. Check water level, adding more if necessary.
Remove the chicken. Add the carrots, the chicken stock, the lemon and parsley to the sauce. Simmer. At the last moment, add the chicken to heat, and the olive oil.
Serve in 40 cm diameter plate and decorate with the red olives.

Poulet a la Vapeur farci de Vermicelle de Riz, de Foie et Garni de Légumes

Steamed chicken with a filling of Chinese noodles and liver and a vegetable accompaniment

Difficulty: ✳✳✳

Preparation time: 1 h 30 min

Casablanca: "United Nations Square".

PREPARATION

Soak the Chinese noodles in water. Fry the liver with a little salt and pepper in a frying pan with a little oil, then dice and place liver in a salad bowl.

Break up the mince in a frying pan and fry it in a little oil. Add the liver.

Drain the noodles, slice and add to the above preparation. Add the spices, the crystallised lemon and the parsley and stir well. Stuff the chickens with this mixture.

Place water in the lower couscous pan and the chickens in the upper pan with the vegetables. Add salt and pepper and the mint. Boil for one half an hour, more or less.

Melt the butter with the stock cube and spread the chickens with this mixture. Bake lightly in over.

Place the chickens on a 50 cm diameter plate, the necks towards the centre and decorate with the vegetables as in the photograph.

Ingredients for 6 people:

3 chickens
250 g Chinese noodles
250 g small carrots, peeled and finely sliced
250 g potatoes, peeled and finely sliced
250 g green beans
A few sprigs of mint
1 green salad
150 g mince
150 g chicken liver
4 cloves garlic
1 sprig chopped parsley
The peel from one crystallised lemon, sliced
1 teaspoonful pepper
1 teaspoonful salt
Pinch of artificial colouring
1 chicken stock cube
75 g butter

La Dinde de la Ferme farcie
Stuffed turkey

Filling:

In a bowl, moisten the semolina with the orange blossom water and the water. Add salt and oil. Stir carefully and steam in the couscous pan for 30 minutes.

Meanwhile, grind the 200 g almonds and place in a recipient with the raisins, washed and dried. Add pepper, cinnamon and sugar.

In a frying pan, blend the chicken stock cube in butter and add this to the mixture above.

After 30 minutes, pour the semolina onto the filling mixture and stir well.

Use this mixture to stuff the turkey. Sew up the opening so that the stuffing does not spill out. Tie the turkey's legs.

Cooking the turkey:

In a pressure cooker, lightly fry the onions in oil for around 5 minutes. Meanwhile, crush the garlic in a mortar, adding the spices.

Spread this mixture over the turkey and place in the pan, on top of the sautéed onions. Add the butter and the stock cube. Simmer for 2 or 3 minutes.

Add a litre and a half of water. Cover the pan and simmer for around 75 minutes.

Check that the turkey is cooked and remove. Bake in the oven for around 15 minutes. Reduce the sauce. Carefully clean the dates with a dry cloth and spread with oil.

Serve the turkey on a round tray. Pour sauce around it and decorate with the dates, stuffed with toasted almonds.

Difficulty: ✳✳✳

Preparation: 2 h 40 min

Ingredients for 8 people:

1 turkey, weighing around 5 kg
2 large onions, diced
6 cloves garlic
1 teaspoonful powdered ginger
Pinch of artificial colouring
10 strands natural saffron
1 teaspoonful salt
1 tablespoonful sweet paprika
50 g butter
1/2 small cup cooking oil
1 chicken stock cube

For the filling:
500 g semolina
200 g almonds, boiled and peeled
150 g seedless red raisins
2 tablespoons powdered sugar
1/2 teaspoonful salt
1/2 teaspoonful powdered pepper
1 teaspoonful powdered cinnamon
1 chicken stock cube
1 spoonful butter
1/2 small cup cooking oil
1/2 small cup orange blossom water
1/2 small cup water

For the decoration:
200 g peeled almonds, toasted in oil
20 dates, stoned, preferably majhoul
1 tablespoonful oil

Pigeons Kedra aux Amandes et aux Oignons

Pigeon Kedra with almonds and onions

Difficulty. ✱✱

Preparation time: 1 h 30 min

Ingredients for 6 people:

12 pigeons, drawn (entrails removed) and cleaned
200 g rice
1 kg white onions, finely sliced
1 sprig coriander
1 teaspoonful pepper
1 teaspoonful salt
2 sprigs cinnamon
1 chicken stock cube
Pinch of artificial colouring
or sheep's milk butter
1 tablespoonful butter (Smen)
1 small cup olive oil
600 g almonds

PREPARATION

Boil water in a pan. Boil the almonds for around 5 minutes, when they should be easy to peel. Remove from heat, cool them under the cold water tap and peel.
Place the pigeons in a pan with the butter, the cinnamon, the pepper, the salt, the colouring and half the chicken stock cube, and sauté.

Add 1/3 of the onions and half the almonds. Sauté. Cover with water and boil for 45 minutes with the lid on, checking the water level and adding more if necessary. Remove the pigeons once cooked. Put aside a little liquid from this pan. In the remaining stock, add the onions, the coriander and the other half of the chicken stock cube. Simmer for around 20 minutes. Reduce the sauce. Finally, add the olive oil and heat the pigeons in the pan once more.

In a small saucepan, place the stock put aside, with a little colouring and pepper and salt. Add the rice and cover, boiling for around 20 minutes. In a frying pan gently fry the almonds with a little oil. Place the rice in a bowl and the bowl in the centre of a tray. Place the pigeons around the bowl. Sprinkle with the onion sauce. Decorate with the toasted almonds.

79

Rouleau farcis à la viande hachée - « Knanetes »

Knanetes (Roll stuffed with minced meat)

PREPARATION

In a pan, gently fry the onions in 50 g butter for 10 minutes.

Add minced meat and gently fry mixture until the meat breaks up and absorbs all the sauce.

In another pan, fry the kidneys with the remaining butter and the garlic. Add pepper and simmer for 5-10 minutes.

Remove kidneys and add to minced meat. Put this sauce by.

Add to this sauce the mushrooms, the parsley and the mustard and crumble the meat extract into it. Simmer until sauce is absorbed.

Add this preparation to the first mixture.

Add spicy sauce and the ingredient for the stuffing and allow to cool.

Beat egg and flour to make a paste.

Using kitchen scissors, cut puff pastry into four quarters.

Take one quarter spread it out and place a tablespoonful of the stuffing onto the outer edge. Join the two edges and roll inwards. Join ends with a little paste.

Repeat the operation with the other leaves of puff pastry.

Difficulty: ✷✷

Preparation time: 2 h

Ingredients for 10 or 12 people:

600 g minced beef, seasoned
1 beef kidney, finely sliced
300 g pickled mushrooms, sliced
5 cloves garlic, chopped
3 onions, diced
3 dessertspoonfuls parsley, finely chopped
1 tablespoonful mustard (sweet)
1/2 teaspoonful pepper
70 g butter
1 meat extract
750 g puff pastry leaves (35-40 cm diameter)
1 egg
1 tablespoonful flour
Spicy sauce to taste

Cooking options:

To bake: grease rolls with butter before place in oven (200°) for 30 or 40 minutes.

To fry: heat oil and fry rolls one by one. Remove and drain on kitchen roll.

Serve accompanied by mint tea.

Ghraïfs farcis aux Oignons et Khlii

Ghraïfs stuffed with onion and khlii

Difficulty: ✳✳

Preparation time: 2 h

Fes: Bab el Mahrouk.

Ingredients for 6 people:

<u>For the dough:</u>
500 g flour
1 teaspoonful salt
A little lukewarm water
1 large cup cooking oil

<u>For the filling:</u>
1.5 kg onions, chopped
1 red pepper and 1 green pepper, chopped
200 g khlii* with little fat, chopped
100 g agriche
4 tablespoons chopped parsley
1 teaspoonful pepper
salt to taste

PREPARATION

In a deep frying pan, sauté the onions with the khlii and the agriche. Add the peppers, the parsley and the pepper. Sauté and reduce the sauce. Allow to cool.
Stir the flour and the salt into the lukewarm water, and knead into a uniform dough, making balls the size of table tennis balls.
Soak in oil and leave to rest in a dish.
Roll out each ball to make biscuits. Spread a spoonful of filling in the centre of each and fold sides inwards to form squares. Allow to rest. Gently flatten the ghraïfs and fry on either side in the deep pan.
Serve with mint tea.

* To prepare the khlii, see page 44.

Tagine de Courgettes et de Gombos

Courgette and okra tagine

Ingredients for 8 people:

1 kg small green courgettes

200 g okra (a green pepper spice)

3 small red onions, sliced

8 shallots

2 large tomatoes

1 red pepper

2 Italian green peppers

4 cloves garlic

150 g khlii*, without fat, sliced

3 tablespoons chopped parsley

1/2 teaspoonful pepper

1/2 teaspoonful salt

Pinch of artificial colouring

1 stock cube

2 tablespoons khlii* fat

Difficulty: ✳

Preparation time: 40 min

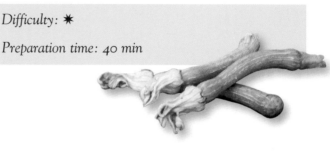

PREPARATION

In a tagine, arrange the courgettes, washed and dice. Add the sliced onions and the shallots, peeled.
Peel the tomatoes, remove the pips and dice. Crush the garlic.
Remove the head from the washed okra.
Cut the pepper into slices.
Add salt, pepper, colouring and the beef stock cube.
Pour on the khlii fat.
Decorate with the pieces of khlii and the green peppers.
Sprinkle with parsley and add a little water.
Cover and simmer for around 35 minutes.
Check cooking and add water if necessary.
Serve hot.

*Khlii or kadide: dry, salted lamb, conserved in lamb's fat.

Zagora: Kasbah Asmaa.

Tagine de Fèves à l'Huile d'Olives

Bean tagine with olive oil

Difficulty: ✳

Preparation time: 15 min

Ouarzazate. the Taourirt Kasbah.

Ingredients for 6 people:

3 kg broad beans

1 tomato

Grated crystallised lemon

4 cloves garlic

3 tablespoons coriander, crushed

1 red chilli pepper

1 teaspoonful pepper

1 teaspoonful salt

Pinch of artificial colouring

1 beef stock cube

1/2 small cup olive oil

PREPARATION

Peel the beans and remove the top. Make a small cut in each and wash carefully.

In a mortar, crush the coriander, the garlic and the salt. Pour this mixture into a pressure cooker.

Add the beans, the peeled tomato, removing the seeds and cutting into quarters, the lemon peel and the chilli pepper. Add the pepper, the colouring, the stock cube and the oil. Simmer, stirring with a wooden spoon. Cover with 1/2 litre water.

Cover and boil for around 15 minutes until the stock has been reduced by half. Serve hot immediately.

Bissara
(Purée de Fèves)
Bissara (Bean purée)

Difficulty: ✳

Preparation time: 35 min

Chefchaouen:
Outa Hammam square.

Ingredients for 6 people:

1 kg dried beans, peels	1 teaspoonful cumin
4 cloves garlic	1 teaspoonful salt
The juice of one large lemon	1 small cup olive oil
1 teaspoonful paprika	1 litre water

PREPARATION

In a pan, boil the water with the salt, the crushed garlic and the beans. Check water, adding more if necessary.

When cooked, liquidise. Add the lemon juice.

Serve on a soup plate, decorated with olive oil, paprika and cumin.

This is an ideal plate for winter, preferably accompanied by wholemeal bread.

Les Haricots Blancs
Broad beans

Difficulty: ✷✷

Preparation time: 1 h 30 min

Fes:
Bab Boujloud.

Ingredients for 6 people:

500 g broad beans, left to soak overnight

1 medium-sized onion, sliced

1 red pimento, sliced

1 medium-sized tomato, chopped

5 cloves garlic, chopped

2 tablespoons parsley, chopped

1 tablespoons tomato purée

1 teaspoon pepper

1 teaspoon salt

1 pinch saffron

½ glass table oil

½ glass olive oil

1 beef stock cube

PREPARATION

In a pan, place the beans, strained, the onion, the tomato, the pimento, the garlic, the parsley, the tomato purée, both types of oil, the stock cube, salt, pepper and saffron. Over a gentle heat, use a wooden spatula to stir as you add 3/4 litre water. Simmer for 30 or 40 minutes, adding more water if necessary, until you obtain a buttery sauce. Serve hot.

Les Lentilles

Lentils

The Imouzer Waterfall near Agadir.

Difficulty: ✳✳

Preparation time: 1 h 40 min

Ingredients for 6 people:

500 g lentils, left to soak overnight

1 medium-sized onion

1 red pimento, sliced

1 medium-sized tomato, grated

4 cloves garlic, chopped

2 tablespoons fresh coriander, chopped

1 teaspoon pepper

1 teaspoon salt

1 pinch saffron

½ glass table oil

½ glass olive oil

1 beef stock cube

PREPARATION

In a mortar, mash the coriander, the garlic and the salt. Pour this mixture into a pan. Add the lentils, strained, the grated tomato, the onion, sliced, and the pimento.
Next, add pepper, saffron, the stock cube and the oil.
Over a gentle heat, use a wooden spatula to stir as you add ½ litre water. Simmer for 20 minutes. Serve straight away, hot.

Escargots « Ghelale »
Ghelale snails

Difficulty: ✳✳✳

Preparation time: 2 h 30 min

Laayoune.

Ingredients for 8 or 10 people:

3 kg live striped snails

2 tablespoonfuls caraway seeds

3 tablespoonfuls thyme

1 tablespoonful tea

1 tablespoonful salt

2 tablespoonfuls green anisette

5 roots "aârk-souss" liquorice

5 bay leaves

Half the peel of a dried pomegranate

The fresh peel of a bitter orange

6 small sprigs fresh mint

5 red peppers

1,5 g gum Arabic

100 g bran

PREPARATION

Place the snails with the bran in a clean plastic bowl and leave them overnight to feed, purging them. Cover the bowl with a kitchen cloth to stop the snails from getting out.

When ready to prepare the dish, wash snails well in salted water, rinsing several times. Place in 5-6 litres of boiling water and cook for 10 minutes. Skim off foam with a soup spoon.

Place all the spices on a very fine cloth, tie and place at the bottom of the pan. Simmer snails for 2 hours, checking the water from time to time and stirring to ensure that they are evenly cooked. Salt to taste.

There should be plenty of stock once cooked.

Serve stock hot or cold in bowls, using an escargot fork to remove snails from shells.

95

CONTENTS

PRESENTATION 1
INTRODUCTION 3
MINT TEA 5

STARTERS
Chicken b'stilla pie 6
Seafood b'stilla (pie) 8
Classical Lahrira Fassia 10

MEAT
Lamb méchoui...................................12
Tfaia
(lamb with almonds and eggs) 14
Lamb Lmhammar 16
Mrozia tagine 18
Tagine of Veal with prunes...................20
Berber Tagine with seven vegetables...........22
Lamb tagine with artichoke hearts 24
Beef tagine with ground olives 26
Beef tagine with Brussels sprouts
and carrots 28
Beef tagine with green beans..................30
Mahfour (beef tagine with turnips) 32
Beef tagine with quince and okra...............34
Medfouna with meat 36
Beef kebabs 38
Maghdour Tagine Kebabs 40
Khlii 42
Kadide (mince) tagine with tomatoes 44
Veal Tanjia Marrakchia 46

COUSCOUS DISHES
"Makhzani" couscous with seven
vegetables 48
"Tfaya" couscous with raisins and
almonds 50
Brkoukss (Soussi couscous)..................52

Soussi couscous................................54

OFFAL
Tagine of hoof of beef (Hergma)................56
Skhina Tagine 58
Fassia M'chermel liver tagine....................60

FISH
Tagine of stuffed sea trout....................62
Sea bream, stuffed with seafood 64
Sardine tagine 66

POULTRY
M'hammer chicken tagine 68
Beldi M'qalli chicken tagine....................70
Chicken tagine with carrots 72
Steamed chicken with a filling of
Chinese noodles and liver and a vegetable
accompaniment 74
Stuffed turkey 76
Pigeon Kedra with almonds and onions 78

PUFF PASTRY DISHES
Knanetes (Roll stuffed with minced meat) 80
Ghraïfs stuffed with onion and khlii 82

VEGETABLES
Courgette and okra tagine.......................84
Bean tagine with olive oil 86

STARCHY
Bissara (Bean purée) 92
Broad beans 90
Lentils 92

SNAILS
Ghelale snails 94